One, Two, Buckle My Shoe

Retold by Russell Punter

Illustrated by David Semple

Reading consultant: Alison Kelly
Roehampton University

One, two,

buckle my shoe.

Three, four,

knock at the door.

Five, six,

pick up sticks.

Seven, eight,

lay them straight.

Nine, ten,

a big fat hen.

Eleven, twelve,

dig and delve.

Thirteen, fourteen,

maids a-courting.

Fifteen, sixteen,

maids in the kitchen.

Seventeen, eighteen,

maids a-waiting.

Nineteen, twenty,
my plate's empty.

Twenty-one, twenty-two,
"Shoo fox, shoo!"

Twenty-three,
twenty-four,

home once more.

Twenty-five, twenty-six,

"Let's get this fixed."

Twenty-seven,
twenty-eight,

fasten the gate.

Twenty-nine, thirty,

Gertie

"You're safe now,
Gertie."

PUZZLES
Puzzle 1
Can you spot the differences between these two pictures? There are six to find.

Puzzle 2

Choose the best phrase for each picture.

1.

A-Tickle my shoe.

B-Buckle my shoe.

2.

A-A big fat hen.

B-A big fat pen.

Puzzle 3
Put the pictures in order.

A

B

C

D

E

F

Answers to puzzles

Puzzle 1